W9-BRL-578

Little People, BIG DREAMS
AUDREY HEPBURN

Written by
Mª Isabel Sánchez Vegara

Illustrated by
Amaia Arrazola

Frances Lincoln
Children's Books

Little Audrey lived in a town called Arnhem, in the Netherlands. She dreamed of what she would do when she grew up . . . Would she become a ballerina—or maybe an actress?

But one day, on her way to ballet class, Audrey saw soldiers on the streets. War had broken out. She watched many families being sent away from their homes—including children just like her.

It was a hard time for Audrey and all the other children.
There was very little food, and they were often hungry.
Audrey became very ill.

At last the fighting ended, and Audrey moved to London to study dance. Her teacher said she was too weak from the war to become a ballerina. But Audrey didn't give up . . .

She decided to act and dance in musicals instead!

Before long, she was making her first Hollywood film—driving around Rome with the famous actor Gregory Peck!

Every role she played was different from the one before.
One day she was a nun, and the next . . . a princess!

She had a simple rule for life: "Dance as though no one is watching. Sing as though no one can hear you. Live as though heaven is on Earth."

She also liked to spend time alone in her apartment. Every day at breakfast, she read letters from her fans. She was loved by millions of people around the world!

Audrey won award after award. But she worried that she didn't deserve them. While she was a Hollywood star who seemed to have everything . . .

. . . she never forgot that there were children in the world who were hungry, just like she had been.

One day, a charity offered her a new role. They asked her to become their official ambassador and visit children all over the world! So Audrey traveled to India . . .

. . . and to Africa! Wherever she went, Audrey tried to make every child happy. She helped raise money to provide children with water, food, and medicine.

Audrey spent the rest of her life helping people across the globe. And that made her happier than acting or dancing ever had.

AUDREY HEPBURN

(Born 1929 • Died 1993)

1946 (right)   1950

Audrey Hepburn was one of the most iconic actresses of stage
and screen. She was born Audrey Kathleen Ruston in Belgium
in 1929. Her mother, Ella van Heemstra, was a Dutch baroness
and her father, Joseph Ruston, was British. Her parents broke up
when she was three, and Audrey moved with her mother to
Arnhem, a small town in the Netherlands. It was here that
Audrey started to take ballet lessons. When World War Two
broke out in 1939, Audrey's mother hoped that the Netherlands
would be safe. Unfortunately Audrey's family, like many others,
suffered greatly during the war. Food was scarce, and she
witnessed crimes she would remember for the rest of her life.

1956   1991

After the war, Audrey trained to be a ballerina, moving to
London to study at the famous Rambert School of Ballet. But she
was weak from years of malnutrition, so she decided to focus on
acting instead of ballet. She got her big break in the Broadway
play *Gigi*, and went on to star in many Hollywood films, such as
Breakfast at Tiffany's, winning prestigious awards. During her
retirement, the children's charity UNICEF asked her to be their
Goodwill Ambassador. She traveled all around the world, raising
awareness for children who needed food, clean water, and
medicine. Audrey did whatever she could to help others, because
she remembered how she had felt when she was a child in need.

Want to find out more about **Audrey Hepburn**?

Read this great book:

Just Being Audrey by Margaret Cardillo

You could also watch one of her many films, such as *My Fair Lady*

or *Roman Holiday.*

Quarto is the authority on a wide range of topics.

Quarto educates, entertains and enriches the lives of our readers—enthusiasts and lovers of hands-on living.

www.quartoknows.com

First published in the U.S.A. in 2017 by Frances Lincoln Children's Books,
an imprint of The Quarto Group,
142 W 36th Street, 4th Floor, New York, NY 10018, U.S.A. QuartoKnows.com
Visit our blogs at QuartoKids.com

Text copyright © 2015 by Mª Isabel Sánchez Vegara
Illustrations copyright © 2015 by Amaia Arrazola

First published in Spain in 2015 under the title *Pequeña & Grande Audrey Hepburn*
by Alba Editorial, s.l.u., Baixada de Sant Miquel, 1, 08002 Barcelona
www.albaeditorial.es

ISBN 978-1-78603-053-5

Published by Rachel Williams • Designed by Karissa Santos
Edited by Katy Flint • Production by Kate O'Riordan

Manufactured in Guangdong, China 112018

7 9 8

MIX
Paper from
responsible sources
FSC® C008047

Photographic acknowledgments (pages 28–29, from left to right) 1. Audrey Hepburn with mother, 1946 © Hulton Archive, Getty Images 2.
Audrey Hepburn rehearsing at the barre, 1950 © Silver Screen Collection, Getty Images 3. Audrey Hepburn in Funny Face, 1956 © Mondadori
Portfolio, Getty Images 4. UNICEF Gala honoring Audrey Hepburn, 1991 © Ron Galella, Getty Images

Collect the *Little People,* **BIG DREAMS** series:

FRIDA KAHLO

ISBN: 978-1-84780-783-0

COCO CHANEL

ISBN: 978-1-84780-784-7

MAYA ANGELOU
ISBN: 978-1-84780-889-9

AMELIA EARHART
ISBN: 978-1-84780-888-2

AGATHA CHRISTIE

ISBN: 978-1-78603-220-1

MARIE CURIE

ISBN: 978-1-84780-962-9

ROSA PARKS

ISBN: 978-1-78603-018-4

AUDREY HEPBURN
ISBN: 978-1-78603-053-5

EMMELINE PANKHURST
ISBN: 978-1-78603-020-7

ELLA FITZGERALD

ISBN: 978-1-78603-087-0

ADA LOVELACE

ISBN: 978-1-78603-076-4

JANE AUSTEN

ISBN: 978-1-78603-120-4

GEORGIA O'KEEFFE

ISBN: 978-1-78603-122-8

HARRIET TUBMAN

ISBN: 978-1-78603-227-0

ANNE FRANK

ISBN: 978-1-78603-229-4

MOTHER TERESA

ISBN: 978-1-78603-230-0

JOSEPHINE BAKER

ISBN: 978-1-78603-228-7

L. M. MONTGOMERY

ISBN: 978-1-78603-233-1

JANE GOODALL

ISBN: 978-1-78603-231-7

SIMONE DE BEAUVOIR

ISBN: 978-1-78603-232-4

Now in board book format:

COCO CHANEL

ISBN: 978-1-78603-245-4

MAYA ANGELOU
ISBN: 978-1-78603-249-2

FRIDA KAHLO

ISBN: 978-1-78603-247-8

AMELIA EARHART

ISBN: 978-1-78603-251-5

MARIE CURIE

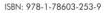
ISBN: 978-1-78603-253-9